SAINT JOSEPH

PRAYER BOOK

V. He made him the lord of his household;
R. And prince over all his possessions.

—*Psalm 105:21*

SAINT JOSEPH
FOSTER FATHER OF OUR LORD JESUS CHRIST
MOST CHASTE SPOUSE OF THE
BLESSED VIRGIN MARY

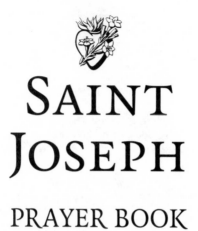

SAINT JOSEPH

PRAYER BOOK

Compiled from Traditional Sources

"ITE AD JOSEPH."
"Go to Joseph."
(Genesis 41:55)

TAN Books
Gastonia, North Carolina

Nihil Obstat: Reverend Matthew Kauth, STD
                 Censor Deputatus

Imprimatur: Most Reverend Peter J. Jugis, JCD
                 Bishop of Charlotte
                 January 1, 2020
                 Solemnity of Mary, the Holy Mother of God

Cover illustration and design by Caroline Green. Photo on page 73 copyright Daprato Statuary Co.

Library of Congress Catalog Card No.: 91-65847

ISBN: 978-1-5051-1679-3

This booklet was published in large part through the help of Ed Desloge.

Published in the United States by
TAN Books
PO Box 269
Gastonia, NC 28053
www.TANBooks.com

Printed in the United States of America

Go to Joseph!

"Of old it was said to the needy and suffering people in the kingdom of Egypt: 'Go to Joseph, and do all that he shall say to you.' (*Gen.* 41:55).

"The same is now said by the Sovereign Pontiff to all needy and suffering people in the kingdom of the Church: Go to Joseph. . . .

"What was truly said of the first Joseph, as to his future, and as to his goodness, his chastity, his patience, his wisdom, his influence with the king, his power over the people, and his love for his brethren, is verified much more perfectly, even to this day, in the second Joseph."

—*Herbert Cardinal Vaughan*
Archbishop of Westminster

CONTENTS

1

FOREWORD

Dear Brothers and Sisters in Christ,

Grace to you and peace from God our Father and the Lord Jesus Christ.

A very significant moment in the Church's history of devotion to Saint Joseph occurred in 1870 when Blessed Pope Pius IX solemnly proclaimed Saint Joseph to be the Patron of the Catholic Church.

We wish to honor Saint Joseph, this holy patron and protector of the Universal Church, on the 150th anniversary of that solemn proclamation by Blessed Pope Pius IX, by celebrating the year 2020 as The Year of Saint Joseph in the Diocese of Charlotte.

The Saint Joseph Prayer Book you have before you contains spiritual treasures from the Church's venerable tradition of devotion to Saint Joseph.

Saint Joseph is a model of holiness for each and every member of the Church, as Pope Saint

5

John Paul II reminded us in his apostolic exhortation, *Redemptoris Custos*: "Besides trusting in Joseph's sure protection, the Church also trusts in his noble example, which transcends all individual states of life and serves as a model for the entire Christian community, whatever the condition and duties of each of its members may be."

May the prayers in this Saint Joseph Prayer Book help you grow in holiness, and deepen your devotion to Saint Joseph. May these prayers also deepen your devotion to his most holy spouse, the Blessed Virgin Mary, and lead you closer to Jesus our Lord.

Saint Joseph, Spouse of the Mother of God and Foster Father of the Son of God, pray for us.

Sincerely yours in Christ,

Most Reverend Peter J. Jugis
Bishop of Charlotte
January 1, 2020
The Year of Saint Joseph

PRAYER TO ST. JOSEPH
BY POPE LEO XIII

TO YOU, O blessed Joseph,
do we come in our afflictions,
and having implored the help of your most holy
Spouse,
we confidently invoke your patronage also.

Through that charity which bound you
to the Immaculate Virgin Mother of God
and through the paternal love
with which you embraced the Child Jesus,
we humbly beg you graciously to regard the inheritance
which Jesus Christ has purchased by his Blood,
and with your power and strength to aid us in our
necessities.
O most watchful guardian of the Holy Family,
defend the chosen children of Jesus Christ;
O most loving father, ward off from us
every contagion of error and corrupting influence;

7

O our most mighty protector, be kind to us
and from heaven assist us in our struggle
with the power of darkness.

As once you rescued the Child Jesus from deadly
    peril,
so now protect God's Holy Church
from the snares of the enemy and from all adver-
    sity;
shield, too, each one of us by your constant pro-
    tection,
so that, supported by your example and your aid,
we may be able to live piously, to die in holiness,
and to obtain eternal happiness in heaven.
Amen.

LITANY OF ST. JOSEPH

(For public or private use.)

L ORD, have mercy on us.
  Christ, have mercy on us.
Lord, have mercy on us. Christ, hear us.
 Christ, graciously hear us.
God the Father of Heaven,
 Have mercy on us.
God the Son, Redeemer of the world,
 Have mercy on us.
God the Holy Ghost,
 Have mercy on us.
Holy Trinity, One God,
 Have mercy on us.

Holy Mary, *pray for us.*
St. Joseph, *pray for us.*
Illustrious son of David, *etc.*
Light of patriarchs,
Spouse of the Mother of God,
Chaste guardian of the Virgin,
Foster father of the Son of God,
Watchful defender of Christ,
Head of the Holy Family,

Joseph most just,
Joseph most chaste,
Joseph most prudent,
Joseph most valiant,
Joseph most obedient,
Joseph most faithful,
Mirror of patience,
Lover of poverty,
Model of workmen,
Glory of home life,
Guardian of virgins,
Pillar of families,
Solace of the afflicted,
Hope of the sick,
Patron of the dying,
Terror of demons,
Protector of Holy Church,

Lamb of God, Who takes away the sins of the world, *Spare us, O Lord!*

Lamb of God, Who takes away the sins of the world, *Graciously hear us, O Lord!*

Lamb of God, Who takes away the sins of the world, *Have mercy on us!*

V.   He made him the lord of His household,

R.   *And prince over all His possessions.*

Let Us Pray

O God, Who in Thine ineffable Providence didst vouchsafe to choose Blessed Joseph to be the spouse of Thy most holy Mother, grant, we beseech Thee, that he whom we venerate as our protector on earth may be our intercessor in Heaven. Who lives and reigns forever and ever. Amen.

NOVENA TO ST. JOSEPH

O GLORIOUS St. Joseph, faithful follower of Jesus Christ, to thee do we raise our hearts and hands to implore thy powerful intercession in obtaining from the benign Heart of Jesus all the helps and graces necessary for our spiritual and temporal welfare, particularly the grace of a happy death, and the special favor we now implore (*state your petition*).

O Guardian of the Word Incarnate, we have confidence that thy prayers on our behalf will be graciously heard before the throne of God. Amen.

(Then say the following seven times in honor of the seven sorrows and joys of St. Joseph.)

V. O Glorious St. Joseph! Through thy love for Jesus Christ and for the glory of His Name,
R. *Hear our prayers and obtain our petitions.*
V. Jesus, Mary and Joseph,
R. *Assist us!*

MEMORARE TO ST. JOSEPH

REMEMBER, O most pure Spouse of the Virgin Mary, St. Joseph my beloved patron, that never has it been heard that anyone invoked thy patronage and sought thine aid without being comforted. Inspired by this confidence, I come to thee and fervently commend myself to thee. Ah, despise not my petition, dear Foster Father of our Redeemer, but accept it graciously. Amen.

The Testimony of St. Teresa

Words of St. Teresa of Avila

"I took for my patron and lord the glorious St. Joseph, and recommended myself earnestly to him. I saw clearly that both out of this my present trouble, and out of others of greater importance, relating to my honor and the loss of my soul, this my father and lord delivered me, and rendered me greater services than I knew how to ask for. I cannot call to mind that I have ever asked him at any time for anything which he has not granted; and I am filled with amazement when I consider the great favors which God has given me through this blessed Saint; the dangers from which he has delivered me, both of body and of soul."

—*Autobiography*, VI, 9

ANOTHER MEMORARE TO ST. JOSEPH

REMEMBER, O most illustrious Patriarch St. Joseph, on the testimony of St. Teresa, thy devoted client, that never has it been heard that anyone invoked thy protection or sought thy mediation who has not obtained relief. In this confidence I come before thee, my loving protector, chaste spouse of Mary, foster father of the Saviour of men and dispenser of the treasures of His Sacred Heart. Despise not my earnest prayer, but graciously hear and obtain my petition. (*Mention your intention.*)

Let Us Pray

O God, Who in Thine ineffable Providence didst vouchsafe to choose Blessed Joseph to be the spouse of Thy most holy Mother, grant, we beseech Thee, that he whom we venerate as our protector on earth may be our intercessor in Heaven. Who lives and reigns forever and ever. Amen.

PRAYER TO OBTAIN A SPECIAL FAVOR

O BLESSED Saint Joseph, tenderhearted father, faithful guardian of Jesus, chaste spouse of the Mother of God, we pray and beseech thee to offer to God the Father His divine Son, bathed in blood on the Cross for sinners, and through the thrice-holy Name of Jesus, obtain for us from the Eternal Father the favor we implore. (*Name your request.*)

Appease the Divine anger so justly inflamed by our crimes, beg of Jesus mercy for thy children.

Amid the splendors of eternity, forget not the sorrows of those who suffer, those who pray, those who weep; stay the Almighty arm which smites us, that by thy prayers and those of thy most holy spouse, the Heart of Jesus may be moved to pity and to pardon. Amen. St. Joseph, pray for us.

Words of St. Thomas Aquinas

"Some Saints are privileged to extend to us their patronage with particular efficacy in certain needs, but not in others; but our holy patron St. Joseph has the power to assist us in all cases, in every necessity, in every undertaking."

St. Teresa's "Guarantee"

Words of St. Teresa of Avila

"To other Saints Our Lord seems to have given power to succor us in some special necessity—but to this glorious Saint, I know by experience, He has given the power to help us in all. Our Lord would have us understand that as He was subject to St. Joseph on earth—for St. Joseph, bearing the title of father and being His guardian, could command Him—so now in Heaven Our Lord grants all his petitions. I have asked others to recommend themselves to St. Joseph, and they, too, know the same thing by experience . . ."

—Autobiography, VI, 9

THIRTY DAYS' PRAYER
TO ST. JOSEPH

For Any Special Intention

EVER BLESSED and glorious St. Joseph, kind and loving father, and helpful friend of all in sorrow! Thou art the good father and protector of orphans, the defender of the defenseless, the patron of those in need and sorrow. Look kindly on my request. My sins have drawn down on me the just displeasure of my God, and so I am surrounded with unhappiness. To thee, O loving guardian of the Family of Nazareth, do I go for help and protection.

Listen, then, I beg of thee, with fatherly concern, to my earnest prayers, and obtain for me the favor I ask. (*Here make your request.*)

I ask it by the infinite mercy of the Eternal Son of God, which moved Him to take our nature and to be born into this world of sorrow.

I ask it by the weariness and suffering thou didst endure when thou didst find no shelter at the inn of Bethlehem for the Holy Virgin, nor a place where the Son of God could be born. Then, being everywhere refused, thou hadst to allow the Queen of

Heaven to give birth to the world's Redeemer in a cave.

I ask it by the loveliness and power of that sacred Name, Jesus, which thou didst confer on the adorable Infant.

I ask it by that painful torture thou didst feel at the prophecy of holy Simeon, which declared the Child Jesus and His holy Mother future victims of our sins and of their great love for us.

I ask it through thy sorrow and pain of soul when the Angel declared to thee that the life of the Child Jesus was sought by His enemies. From their evil plan thou hadst to flee with Him and His Blessed Mother into Egypt. I ask it by all the suffering, weariness and labors of that long and dangerous journey.

I ask it by all thy care to protect the Sacred Child and His Immaculate Mother during thy second journey, when thou wert ordered to return to thine own country. I ask it by thy peaceful life in Nazareth, where thou didst meet with so many joys and sorrows.

I ask it by thy great distress when the adorable Child was lost to thee and His Mother for three days. I ask it by thy joy at finding Him in the Temple, and by the comfort thou didst find at Nazareth, while living in the company of the Child Jesus. I ask it by the wonderful submission He showed in His obedience to thee.

I ask it by the perfect love and conformity thou didst show in accepting the Divine order to depart from this life and from the company of Jesus and Mary. I ask it by the joy which filled thy soul when the Redeemer of the world, triumphant over death and Hell, entered into the possession of His kingdom and led thee into it with special honors.

I ask it through Mary's glorious Assumption and through that endless happiness thou hast with her in the presence of God.

O good Father! I beg of thee, by all thy sufferings, sorrows and joys, to hear me and obtain for me what I ask. (*Here mention your petitions or think of them.*)

Obtain for all those who have asked my prayers everything that is useful to them in the plan of God. Finally, my dear Patron and Father, be with me and all who are dear to me in our last moments, that we may eternally sing the praises of

Jesus, Mary and Joseph!

A blameless life, O St. Joseph, may we lead, by thy kind patronage from danger freed. Amen.

PRAYER FOR PURITY

O GUARDIAN of Virgins and holy Father St. Joseph, into whose faithful keeping were entrusted Christ Jesus, Innocence itself, and Mary, Virgin of virgins, I pray and beseech thee by these dear pledges, Jesus and Mary, that, being preserved from all uncleanness, I may with spotless mind, pure heart and chaste body ever serve Jesus and Mary most chastely all the days of my life. Amen.

St. Teresa's Plea

Words of St. Teresa of Avila

"Would that I could persuade all men to be devoted to this glorious Saint [St. Joseph], for I know by long experience what blessings he can obtain for us from God. I have never known anyone who was truly devoted to him and honored him by particular services who did not advance greatly in virtue: for he helps in a special way those souls who commend themselves to him. It is now very many years since I began asking him for something on his feast, and I have always received it. If the petition was in any way amiss, he rectified it for my greater good . . . I ask for the love of God that he who does not believe me will make the trial for himself—then he will find out by experience the great good that results from commending oneself to this glorious Patriarch and in being devoted to him . . ."

—Autobiography, VI, 11-12

PRAYER TO ST. JOSEPH THE WORKMAN

Composed by Pope St. Pius X

O GLORIOUS St. Joseph, model of all those who are devoted to labor, obtain for me the grace to work conscientiously, putting the call of duty above my natural inclinations, to work with gratitude and joy, in a spirit of penance for the remission of my sins, considering it an honor to employ and develop by means of labor the gifts received from God, to work with order, peace, moderation and patience, without ever shrinking from weariness and difficulties, to work above all with purity of intention and detachment from self, having always death before my eyes and the account that I must render of time lost, of talents wasted, of good omitted, of vain complacency in success, so fatal to the work of God. All for Jesus, all through Mary, all after thine example, O Patriarch, St. Joseph. Such shall be my watchword in life and in death. Amen.

Words of St. Teresa of Avila

On St. Joseph and Those Devoted to Prayer

"Those persons who give themselves to prayer should in a special manner always have great devotion to St. Joseph, for I know not how anyone can think of the Queen of Angels during the time that she suffered so much with the Infant Jesus without giving thanks to St. Joseph for the assistance he rendered to them then. He who cannot find anyone to teach him how to pray, let him take this glorious Saint for his guide, and he will not lose his way."

—*Autobiography*, VI, 12

A POWERFUL NOVENA TO ST. JOSEPH

This novena has proven to be highly efficacious. It seems to be pleasing to St. Joseph and helpful to souls.

This form of novena was originally devised by the celebrated Fr. Louis Lallemant, S.J. (1587-1633). It has proved particularly effective in obtaining favors through the intercession of St. Joseph. In the *Life* of this saintly priest and great master of the spiritual life, to whom St. Joseph never refused anything he asked, the story is told that on one occasion he urged two young priests to make this novena, promising that they would obtain everything they asked through the intercession of St. Joseph if, in turn, they would show him special honor and spread devotion to him among others.

Both did as Fr. Lallemant suggested. One of them asked for grace to speak and write worthily of Our Lord. But the next day he came to Fr. Lallemant to tell him that, upon reflection, he wished to ask for a different grace, which he considered more conducive to his perfection. Fr. Lallemant replied, "It is too late now to ask for another grace. The first one has already been granted." This grace was conspicuously displayed throughout the whole course of the priest's life, as he became one of the most noted preachers and writers of his day.

How to Make this Novena

No particular prayers need be said for this novena. Every day for nine days, turn to St. Joseph in spirit four times during the day and honor him in the following four points. (These "visits" may be made anywhere—at home, at work, on the street, in the car or bus—and at any time.)

1. During the first visit, consider **St. Joseph's fidelity to grace**. Reflect upon the action of the Holy Ghost in his soul. At the conclusion of this brief meditation, thank God for so honoring St. Joseph, and ask, through his intercession, for a similar grace.

2. Later in the day, consider **St. Joseph's fidelity to the interior life**. Study his spirit of recollection. Think, thank God, and ask.

3. Later still, consider **St. Joseph's love for Our Lady**. Think, thank God, and ask.

4. Finally, in a fourth visit, reflect upon **St. Joseph's love for the Divine Child**. Think, thank God, and ask.

Prayer Which May Be Said at The Conclusion of the Visits

(These prayers are adapted from Reflections for a Novena to St. Joseph, by Sister Emily Joseph, C.S.J.)

O MY GOD, I thank Thee and bless Thee for St. Joseph's great faithfulness to grace. Grant that, through his loving intercession and the power of his example, I too may be faithful to grace.

O St. Joseph, intercede for me, and obtain for me the favor I ask. (*Name your request.*)

O MY GOD, I thank Thee and bless Thee for St. Joseph's great faithfulness to the interior life. Grant that, through his loving intercession and the power of his example, I too may be faithful to the interior life.

O St. Joseph, intercede for me, and obtain for me the favor I ask. (*Name your request.*)

O MY GOD, I thank Thee and bless Thee for St. Joseph's great love for Our Lady. Grant that, through his loving intercession and the power of his example, I too may truly love the Blessed Virgin Mary.

O St. Joseph, intercede for me, and obtain the favor I ask. (*Name your request.*)

O MY GOD, I thank Thee and bless Thee for St. Joseph's great love for the Divine Child. Grant that, through his loving intercession and the power of his example, I too may truly love the Child Jesus.

O St. Joseph, intercede for me, and obtain the favor I ask. (*Name your request.*)

Words of Our Lady to Ven. Mary of Agreda

"The children of the world are ignorant regarding the privileges and rights which the Most High has conferred on my holy spouse, and the power of his intercession with the Divine Majesty and with me. But I assure you, my daughter, that in Heaven he is most intimate with the Lord, and has great power to avert the punishment of Divine justice from sinners. *In all trials seek his intercession, because the Heavenly Father will grant whatever my spouse asks.*"

"On the Day of Judgment, the condemned will weep bitterly for not having realized how powerful and efficacious a means of salvation they might have had in the intercession of St. Joseph, and for not having done their utmost to gain the friendship of the Eternal Judge."

PRAYER TO OBTAIN A CONVERSION

O GLORIOUS PATRIARCH St. Joseph, who merited to be called "just" by the Holy Ghost, I urgently recommend to thee the soul of (*Name*), which Jesus redeemed at the price of His Precious Blood.

Thou knowest how deplorable is the state and how unhappy the life of those who have banished this loving Saviour from their hearts, and how greatly they are exposed to the danger of losing Him eternally. Permit not, I beseech thee, that a soul so dear to me should continue any longer in its evil ways; preserve it from the danger that threatens it; touch the heart of this prodigal child and conduct him back to the bosom of the fondest of fathers.

Abandon him not, I implore thee, till thou hast opened to him the gates of the heavenly city, where he will praise and bless thee throughout eternity for the happiness which he will owe to thy powerful intercession. Amen.

TO THEE, O BLESSED JOSEPH

To be prayed especially after the Rosary.
This prayer is sometimes called the "October Prayer
to St. Joseph," but it can be prayed at any time of year.

TO THEE, O blessed Joseph, do we have recourse in our tribulation, and having implored the help of thy thrice-holy Spouse, we confidently invoke thy patronage also.

By that charity wherewith thou wast united to the Immaculate Virgin Mother of God, and by that fatherly affection with which thou didst embrace the Child Jesus, we beseech thee and we humbly pray that thou wouldst look graciously upon the inheritance which Jesus Christ has purchased by His blood, and assist us in our needs by thy power and strength.

Most watchful Guardian of the Holy Family, protect the chosen people of Jesus Christ. Keep far from us, most loving Father, all blight of error and corruption. Mercifully assist us from Heaven, most mighty defender, in this our conflict with the powers of darkness; and even as of old thou didst rescue the Child Jesus from the supreme peril of His life, so now defend God's holy Church from the snares of the enemy and from all adversity. Keep us one and all under thy continual protection, that, supported by thine example and thine assistance, we may be enabled to live a holy life, die a happy death, and come at last to the possession of everlasting blessedness in Heaven. Amen.

The Seven Sorrows and Seven Joys of St. Joseph

1. The doubt of St. Joseph. (*Matt.* 1:19). The message of the Angel. (*Matt.* 1:20).

2. The poverty of Jesus' birth. (*Luke* 2:7). The birth of the Saviour. (*Luke* 2:7).

3. The Circumcision. (*Luke* 2:21). The Holy Name of Jesus. (*Matt.* 1:25).

4. The prophecy of Simeon. (*Luke* 2:34). The effects of the Redemption. (*Luke* 2:34).

5. The flight into Egypt. (*Matt.* 2:14). The overthrow of the idols of Egypt. (*Is.* 19:1).

6. The return from Egypt. (*Matt.* 2:22). Life with Jesus and Mary at Nazareth. (*Luke* 2:39).

7. The loss of the Child Jesus. (*Luke* 2:45). The finding of the Child Jesus in the Temple. (*Luke* 2:46).

THE DEVOTION OF THE SEVEN SUNDAYS

The Seven Sundays in honor of St. Joseph are observed in the following manner: Holy Communion is received in his honor on seven consecutive Sundays, and on each Sunday the prayers in honor of the Seven Sorrows and the Seven Joys of St. Joseph are recited.

An excellent means of obtaining special favors through the intercession of St. Joseph is to honor his seven sorrows and seven joys by the devotion of the Seven Sundays. This devotion may be practiced at any time of the year, but fervent clients of St. Joseph like to venerate him especially on the seven Sundays preceding his feast. Then they more confidently hope to obtain some particular favor; often the favors they receive are greater than they had expected. St. Teresa of Avila tells us that St. Joseph frequently obtained for her much greater favors than those for which she had petitioned.

It is related that a ship containing a number of passengers was wrecked off the coast of Holland. Two Franciscan monks, who had clung to a plank for two days, were saved by a man of venerable appearance who miraculously brought them to shore. Upon their asking him who he was, he replied, "I am Joseph, and I desire you to honor my seven sorrows and seven joys." This was the origin of the devotion to the sorrows and joys of St. Joseph.

Those who are seeking a special request may also have seven Masses said in honor of St. Joseph, or assist at seven Masses, give alms or fast seven times, make seven visits to a chapel or to an image of the Saint. A novena may be made by daily saying the prayers of the Seven Sorrows and Seven Joys of St. Joseph; or this devotion may be performed for thirty days and ended with the reception of the Sacraments. One can also make a novena by saying the *Our Father, Hail Mary* and *Glory Be* seven times on each of seven consecutive Sundays, in honor of the Seven Sorrows and Joys of St. Joseph. It is very pleasing to St. Joseph and a great act of charity to aid, in his honor, those souls in Purgatory who during life practiced special devotion to him. In our various necessities, we might promise St. Joseph that if he comes to our aid we will have one or more Masses said for the Poor Souls, or offer Holy Communion for them.

PRAYERS IN HONOR OF THE SEVEN SORROWS AND JOYS OF ST. JOSEPH

Composed by Ven. Januarius Sarnelli, C.SS.R. (d. 1744)

1. O chaste Spouse of Mary most holy, glorious St. Joseph, great was the trouble and anguish of thy heart when thou wert minded to put away privately thine inviolate Spouse, yet thy joy was unspeakable when the surpassing mystery of the Incarnation was made known to thee by the Angel!

By this sorrow and this joy, we beseech thee to comfort our souls, both now and in the sorrows of our final hour, with the joy of a good life and a holy death after the pattern of thine own, in the arms of Jesus and Mary.

Our Father . . . Hail Mary . . . Glory be . . .

2. O most blessed Patriarch, glorious St. Joseph, who was chosen to be the foster father of the Word made flesh, thy sorrow at seeing the Child Jesus born in such poverty was suddenly changed into heavenly exultation when thou didst hear the angelic hymn and beheld the glories of that resplendent night.

By this sorrow and this joy, we implore thee to obtain for us the grace to pass over from life's pathway to hear the angelic songs of praise, and to rejoice in the shining splendor of celestial glory.

Our Father . . . Hail Mary . . . Glory be . . .

3. O glorious St. Joseph, thou faithfully obeyed the law of God, and thy heart was pierced at the sight of the Precious Blood that was shed by the Infant Saviour during His Circumcision, but the Name of Jesus gave thee new life and filled thee with quiet joy.

By this sorrow and this joy, obtain for us the grace to be freed from all sin during life, and to die rejoicing, with the holy Name of Jesus in our hearts and on our lips.

Our Father . . . Hail Mary . . . Glory be . . .

4. O most faithful Saint who shared the mysteries of our Redemption, glorious St. Joseph, the prophecy of Simeon regarding the sufferings of Jesus and Mary caused thee to shudder with mortal dread, but at the same time filled thee with a blessed joy for the salvation and glorious resurrection which, he foretold, would be attained by countless souls.

By this sorrow and this joy, obtain for us that we may be among the number of those who, through the merits of Jesus and the intercession of Mary the Virgin Mother, are predestined to a glorious resurrection.

Our Father . . . Hail Mary . . . Glory be . . .

5. O most watchful Guardian of the Incarnate Son of God, glorious St. Joseph, what toil was thine in supporting and waiting upon the Son of the most high God, especially in the flight into Egypt! Yet at the same time, how thou didst rejoice to have always near you God Himself, and to see the idols of the Egyptians fall prostrate to the ground before Him.

By this sorrow and this joy, obtain for us the grace of keeping ourselves in safety from the infernal tyrant, especially by flight from dangerous occasions; may every idol of earthly affection fall from our hearts; may we be wholly employed in serving Jesus and Mary, and for them alone may we live and happily die.

Our Father . . . Hail Mary . . . Glory be . . .

6. O glorious St. Joseph, an angel on earth, thou didst marvel to see the King of Heaven obedient to thy commands, but thy consolation in bringing Jesus out of the land of Egypt was troubled by thy fear of Archelaus; nevertheless, being assured by the Angel, thou dwelt in gladness at Nazareth with Jesus and Mary.

By this sorrow and this joy, obtain for us that our hearts may be delivered from harmful fears, so that we may rejoice in peace of conscience and may live in safety with Jesus and Mary and may, like thee, die in their company.

Our Father . . . Hail Mary . . . Glory be . . .

7. O glorious St. Joseph, pattern of all holiness, when thou didst lose, through no fault of thine own, the Child Jesus, thou sought Him sorrowing for the space of three days, until with great joy thou didst find Him again in the Temple, sitting in the midst of the doctors.

By this sorrow and this joy, we supplicate thee, with our hearts upon our lips, to keep us from ever having the misfortune to lose Jesus through mortal sin; but if this supreme misfortune should befall us, grant that we may seek Him with unceasing sorrow until we find Him again, ready to show us His great mercy, especially at the hour of death; so that we may pass over to enjoy His presence in Heaven; and there, in company with thee, may we sing the praises of His Divine mercy forever.

Our Father . . . Hail Mary . . . Glory be . . .

Antiphon. And Jesus Himself was beginning his

public life about the age of thirty years, being (as it was supposed) the Son of Joseph (Luke 3:23).

V.   Pray for us, O holy Joseph,
R.   That we may be made worthy of the promises of Christ.

Let Us Pray

O God, Who in Thine ineffable Providence didst vouchsafe to choose Blessed Joseph to be the spouse of Thy most holy Mother, grant, we beseech Thee, that he whom we venerate as our protector on earth may be our intercessor in Heaven. Who lives and reigns forever and ever. Amen.

PRAYER AND PROMISE TO ST. JOSEPH

By St. Alphonsus Liguori

O HOLY PATRIARCH, I rejoice with thee at the exalted dignity by which thou wast deemed worthy to act as father to Jesus, to give Him orders and to be obeyed by Him whom Heaven and earth obey.

O great Saint, as thou wast served by God, I too wish to be taken into thy service. I choose thee, after Mary, to be my chief advocate and protector. I promise to honor thee every day by some special act of devotion and by placing myself under thy daily protection. By that sweet company which Jesus and Mary gave thee in thy lifetime, I beseech thee to protect me all through life, so that I may never separate myself from my God by losing His grace.

My dear St. Joseph, pray to Jesus for me. Certainly He can never refuse thee anything, as He obeyed all thine orders while on earth. Tell Him to detach me from all creatures and from myself, to inflame me with His holy love, and then to do with me what He pleases. And by that assistance which Jesus and Mary gave thee at death, I beg of thee to protect me in a special way at the hour of my death, so that dying, assisted by thee, in the company of Jesus and Mary, I may go to thank thee in Paradise, and in thy company praise my God for all eternity. Amen.

Glory be . . . (three times).

PRAYER IN A DIFFICULT PROBLEM

O GLORIOUS St. Joseph, thou who hast power to render possible even things which are considered impossible, come to our aid in our present trouble and distress. Take this important and difficult affair under thy particular protection, that it may end happily. (*Name your request.*)

O dear St. Joseph, all our confidence is in thee. Let it not be said that we would invoke thee in vain; and since thou art so powerful with Jesus and Mary, show that thy goodness equals thy power. Amen.

St. Joseph, friend of the Sacred Heart, pray for us.

AN ANCIENT PRAYER
TO ST. JOSEPH

O ST. JOSEPH, whose protection is so great, so strong, so prompt before the throne of God, I place in thee all my interests and desires.

O St. Joseph, assist me by thy powerful intercession and obtain for me all spiritual blessings through thy foster Son, Jesus Christ Our Lord, so that, having engaged here below thy heavenly power, I may offer thee my thanksgiving and homage.

O St. Joseph, I never weary contemplating thee and Jesus asleep in thine arms. I dare not approach while He reposes near thy heart. Press Him in my name and kiss His fine head for me, and ask Him to return the kiss when I draw my dying breath.

St. Joseph, Patron of departing souls, pray for me.

Publisher's Note: We reproduce here, without comment or guarantee, the following statement which usually accompanies this prayer:

This prayer was found in the fiftieth year of Our Lord and Saviour Jesus Christ. In 1505 it was sent from the Pope to Emperor Charles when he was going into battle. Whoever shall read this prayer or hear it or keep it about themselves shall never die a sudden death or be drowned, nor shall poison take effect on them—neither shall they fall into the hands of the enemy or be burned in any fire or be overpowered in battle.

Say for nine mornings for anything you may desire. It has never been known to fail.

What Must I Do?

What is required of him who venerates St. Joseph as his patron and wishes to obtain favors from him? There are three things:

1. Bring your petitions to St. Joseph in prayer, preferably before an image of him or at an altar or in a church dedicated to him.
2. Have confidence in St. Joseph as your heavenly protector and intercessor.
3. Give thanks to him for the benefits you receive through praying to St. Joseph. Giving thanks is only just; moreover, the returning of thanks gives one a "right," so to speak, to new favors and blessings.

Feasts of St. Joseph

The primary feast of St. Joseph is March 19. It is believed that his death occurred on that day. This feast was fixed in the 15th century and was extended to the whole Church by Pope Gregory XV in 1621. On December 8, 1870, Pope Pius IX ordered that this feast be celebrated throughout the Church as a double of the first class. Holy Church also dedicates to St. Joseph the entire month of March. In addition, pious custom dedicates Wednesday of each week to the honor of St. Joseph.

May 1 was established as the feast of St. Joseph the Workman by Pope Pius XII in 1955. The date was chosen to coincide with the date on which Labor Day is observed in many countries, thus to elevate and sanctify the observance.

Formerly there was a solemnity of the Patronage of St. Joseph which was celebrated each year on the third Sunday after Easter, then changed to the Wednesday following the Second Sunday after Easter, with an octave following. On that day St. Joseph was honored especially as the spouse of the Blessed Virgin Mary and as Patron of the Universal Church. Formerly, there was also a feast of the Espousal of St. Joseph on January 23.

A 16th-Century Prophecy

Isidore of Isolanis, a pious Dominican of the 16th century, prophesied that "the sound of victory" will be heard in the Church Militant "when the faithful recognize the sanctity of St. Joseph." He continues: "The Lord will let His light shine, He will lift the veil, and great men will search out the interior gifts of God that are hidden in St. Joseph; they will find in him a priceless treasure, the like of which they had never found in other saints of the Old Testament. We are inclined to believe that toward the end of time God will overwhelm St. Joseph with glorious honors. If in the past ages, during the storms of persecution, these honors could not be shown to St. Joseph, we must conclude that they have been reserved for later times. *At some future time the feast of St. Joseph will be celebrated as one of the greatest of feasts. The*

Vicar of Christ, inspired by the Holy Spirit, will order this feast to be celebrated in the Universal Church."

PRAYER FOR THE CHURCH MILITANT

Petitions and Dedication to St. Joseph

O GLORIOUS St. Joseph, chosen by God to be the foster father of Jesus, the chaste spouse of Mary ever Virgin and the head of the Holy Family, and then appointed by the Vicar of Christ to be the heavenly patron and defender of the Church founded by Jesus, most confidently do I implore at this moment thy powerful aid for all the Church Militant on earth. Do thou shield with thy truly paternal love especially the Supreme Pontiff and all the bishops and priests who are in union with the Holy See of Peter. Be the defender of all who labor for souls amidst the trials and tribulations of this life, and cause all the peoples of the earth to submit themselves in a docile spirit to that Church which is the ark of salvation for all men.

Be pleased also, dear St. Joseph, to accept this dedication of myself which I now make unto thee.

I dedicate myself wholly to thee, that thou mayest ever be my father, my patron and my guide in the way of salvation. Obtain for me great purity of heart and a fervent devotion to the interior life. Grant that, following thine example, I may direct all my actions to the greater glory of God, in union with the Sacred Heart of Jesus and the Immaculate Heart of Mary and in union with thee. Finally, pray for me that I may be a partaker in the peace and joy which were thine at the hour of thy holy death. Amen.

St. Joseph at Fatima

From Fatima in Lucia's Own Words, pp. 181, 183.
(15th edition, August 2005)

"In October Our Lord will come, as well as Our Lady of Dolors and Our Lady of Carmel. St. Joseph will appear with the Child Jesus to bless the world. . . ." (Words of Our Lady, apparition of September 13, 1917).

"After Our Lady had disappeared into the immense distance of the firmament, we beheld St. Joseph with the Child Jesus and Our Lady robed in white with a blue mantle, beside the sun. St. Joseph and the Child Jesus appeared to bless the world, for they traced the Sign of the Cross with their hands. When, a little later, this apparition disappeared, I saw Our Lord and Our Lady; it seemed to me that it was Our Lady of Dolors. Our Lord appeared to bless the world in the same manner as St. Joseph had done. This apparition also vanished, and I saw Our Lady once more, this time resembling Our Lady of Carmel." (Lucia's description of the vision of October 13, 1917).

PRAYER FOR A PERSON WHO HAS A LABORIOUS OCCUPATION

O BLESSED JOSEPH, who passed thy life in the painful labors of a humble profession, I take thee as my model and my protector. Obtain for me that I may bear patiently the pains and fatigues of my state, so that like thee, sanctifying my labors, I may merit a crown in Heaven. Amen.

PETITIONS FOR
ST. JOSEPH'S BLESSING

BLESS ME, O dearly beloved Father, St. Joseph; bless my body and my soul; bless my resolutions, my words and deeds, all my actions and omissions, my every step; bless all that I possess, all my interior and exterior goods, that all may redound to the greater honor of God. Bless me for time and eternity, and preserve me from every sin.

Obtain for me the grace to make atonement for all my sins by love and contrition here on earth, so that after my last breath I may, without delay, prostrate at thy feet, return thee thanks in Heaven for all the love and goodness thou, O dearest father, hast shown me here below. Amen.

St. Joseph's Patronage

In 1847 Pope Pius IX solemnly proclaimed St. Joseph "Patron and Protector of the Universal Church." And although St. Joseph is our father and our advocate in all necessities, he is especially considered the Patron of a Happy Death, a provider of financial help—particularly to the poor and to religious communities—the patron of families, of laborers, of the sick, of the poor, of the rich (to help them distribute their possessions charitably and to help them attain the riches of Heaven), of the suffering, of travelers, of exiles, of the afflicted, of the married, of virgins, of youths, of priests and of those aspiring to the priesthood, of those advanced in virtue and those devoted to prayer; he is also a rescuer of sinners, consoler and liberator of the Poor Souls, terror of demons and conqueror of Hell. Pope Innocent XI made St. Joseph the patron of the Jesuit missions in China, and Pope Pius XI proclaimed, "We place the vast campaign of the Church against world Communism under the standard of St. Joseph, her mighty protector."

In short, St. Joseph is the Patron and Protector of all classes of Christians.

PRAYER OF MAY 1ST

Collect for the Feast of St. Joseph the Workman

O GOD, the Creator of all things, Who didst frame the law of labor for the human race, graciously grant that, by the example and patronage of St. Joseph, we may do the work Thou dost assign us and earn the reward Thou dost promise. Through Our Lord Jesus Christ, Thy Son, who lives and reigns with Thee in the unity of the Holy Ghost, one God, world without end. Amen.

PRAYER OF ST. CLEMENT MARY HOFBAUER

O ST. JOSEPH, my loving father, I place myself forever under thy protection. Look upon me as thy child, and keep me from all sin. I take refuge in thine arms, so that thou mayest lead me on the path of virtue and assist me at the hour of my death. Amen.

A PRAYER TO ST. JOSEPH FOR THE SUCCESS OF A TEMPORAL AFFAIR

O GREAT ST. JOSEPH, whose influence over the Hearts of Jesus and Mary is all powerful and who hast never been invoked in vain, I ask, with the most firm and lively confidence, the speedy granting of my request. (*State your petition.*)

Dear St. Joseph, obtain for me the object of my prayer if it be for the glory of God and my own salvation; but if it is not, then obtain for me the grace lovingly to resign myself to the Will of my Heavenly

Father, who in the afflictions He permits, as well as in the temporal favors He grants me, has in view only my happiness here and my eternal salvation. Amen.

(Say the Our Father, Hail Mary and Glory be three times to thank God for the privileges bestowed upon St. Joseph.)

PRAYER OF CONFIDENCE

WITH childlike confidence I present myself before thee, O holy Joseph, faithful foster father of Jesus! I beg thy compassionate intercession and support in this, my present necessity. *(Name your petition.)* I firmly believe that thou art most powerful near the throne of God, who chose thee for the foster father of His well-beloved Son, Jesus Christ. O blessed Saint, who saved that Treasure of Heaven, with His virginal Mother, from the fury of His enemies, who with untiring industry supplied His earthly wants and with paternal care accompanied and protected Him in all the journeys of His childhood, take me also, for the love of Jesus, as thy child. Assist me in my present difficulty with thy prayers before God. The infinite goodness of our Saviour, who loved and honored thee as His father upon earth, cannot refuse thee any request now in Heaven.

How many pious souls have sought help from thee in their needs and have experienced, to their joy, how good, how ready thou art to assist. How quickly thou dost turn to those who call upon thee with confidence! How powerful thou art in bringing help and restoring joy to anxious and dejected hearts! Therefore do I fly to thee, O most worthy father of Jesus, most chaste spouse of Mary! Good St. Joseph, I pray thee by the burning love thou hadst for Jesus and Mary upon earth, console me in my distress and present my petition, through Jesus and Mary, before the throne of God! One word from thee will move Him to assist my afflicted soul. Then most joyfully shall I praise Him and thee, and most earnest shall be my thanksgiving! Amen.

(Remember to give thanks to St. Joseph.)

Thanking God for His Gifts to Others

According to St. Gertrude

One of the principles of the spirituality of St. Gertrude, that privileged friend of the Sacred Heart of Jesus, is the following:

When we thank God for graces bestowed on others, with confident hope of receiving the like ourselves, we merit, in some degree, to receive those same gifts ourselves. (See *Love, Peace and Joy* by Very Rev. André Prévot, pp. 175, 103, 104–5).

A PRAYER TO ST. JOSEPH TO KNOW ONE'S VOCATION IN LIFE

O GREAT ST. JOSEPH, so docile to the guidance of the Holy Ghost, obtain for me the grace to know what state of life Divine Providence destines for me. Do not allow me to be deceived with regard to so important a choice, upon which depends my happiness in this world, and even my eternal salvation. Obtain for me that, being enlightened to know the Divine Will and being faithful in accomplishing it, I may embrace that state of life which God has destined for me and which will lead me to a happy eternity. Amen.

PRAISES OF ST. JOSEPH

(These praises may be prayed in thanksgiving for favors received.)

IN the Name of the Father, and of the Son and of the Holy Ghost. Amen.

O holy Patriarch Joseph, ever blessed be thy soul, which was adorned with all the virtues and gifts of the Holy Ghost.
Glory be to the Father . . .

O holy Patriarch Joseph, ever blessed be thine intellect, which was full of the most sublime knowledge of God and was enlightened with revelations.
Glory be to the Father . . .

O holy Patriarch Joseph, ever blessed be thy will, which was all inflamed with love for Jesus and Mary and always perfectly conformable to the Divine will.
Glory be to the Father . . .

O holy Patriarch Joseph, ever blessed be thine eyes, to which it was granted to look continually upon Jesus and Mary.

Glory be to the Father . . .

O holy Patriarch Joseph, ever blessed be thine ears, which merited to hear the sweet words of Jesus and Mary.

Glory be to the Father . . .

O dear St. Joseph, ever blessed be thy tongue, which continually praised God and with profound humility and reverence conversed with Jesus and Mary.

Glory be to the Father . . .

O chaste St. Joseph, ever blessed be thy most pure and loving heart, with which thou didst ardently love Jesus and Mary.

Glory be to the Father . . .

O holy Joseph, ever blessed be thy thoughts, words and actions, each and all of which ever tended to the service of Jesus and Mary.

Glory be to the Father . . .

O holy Patriarch Joseph, ever blessed be all the moments of thy life, which thou didst spend in the service of Jesus and Mary.

Glory be to the Father . . .

O my Protector St. Joseph, ever blessed be that moment of thy life in which thou didst most sweetly die in the arms of Jesus and Mary.

Glory be to the Father . . .

O glorious St. Joseph, ever blessed be that moment in which thou didst enter into the eternal joys of Heaven.

Glory be to the Father . . .

O happy St. Joseph, ever blessed in eternity be every moment in which, until now, in union with all the Saints of Heaven, thou hast enjoyed the incomprehensible bliss of union with God, with Jesus and Mary.

Glory be to the Father . . .

O my dear Protector! Be ever blessed by me and by all creatures, for all eternity, with all the blessings which the Most Holy Trinity bestowed upon thee and with all the benedictions given thee by Jesus and Mary and by the whole Church.

Glory be to the Father . . .

O thrice holy Joseph, blessed in soul and body, in life and death, on earth and in Heaven. Obtain also for me, a poor sinner but nevertheless thy true and faithful client, a share in thy blessings, the grace to imitate thee ardently, and to love and faithfully

serve Jesus, Mary and thyself, and especially the
happiness to die in thy holy arms. Amen.

INVOCATIONS TO ST. JOSEPH

By Father Olier

HAIL JOSEPH, image of God the Father.
Hail Joseph, father of God the Son.
Hail Joseph, temple of the Holy Ghost.
Hail Joseph, beloved of the Holy Trinity.
Hail Joseph, most faithful helper in the great
   plan of Redemption.
Hail Joseph, most worthy spouse of the Virgin
   Mother.
Hail Joseph, father of all the faithful.
Hail Joseph, guardian of holy virgins.
Hail Joseph, greatest lover of poverty.
Hail Joseph, example of meekness and patience.
Hail Joseph, mirror of humility and obedience.
Blessed art thou among all men.
And blessed are thine eyes, which have seen
   what thou hast seen.

And blessed are thine ears, which have heard what
    thou hast heard.

And blessed are thy hands, which have touched
    the Word Incarnate.

And blessed are thine arms, which have carried
    the One who carries all things.

And blessed is thy breast, on which the Son of
    God most sweetly reposed.

And blessed is thy heart, kindled with most ardent
    love.

And blessed be the Eternal Father, who
    chose thee.

And blessed be the Son, who loved thee.

And blessed be the Holy Ghost, who
    sanctified thee.

And blessed be Mary, thy spouse, who loved
    thee as a spouse and a brother.

And blessed be the Angel who guarded thee.

And blessed forever be all who bless thee
    and who love thee.

The Fatherhood of St. Joseph

"And thou shalt call His name Jesus."
—Matthew 1:21

"It belonged to the father to give a name to his son. The angel sent by God to give this mission to Joseph thereby shows that Joseph had with regard to Jesus the same rights as if He were his son."

—St. Andrew Daily Missal, 1952, p. 1214

A PRAYER OF PARENTS TO THE HOLY FAMILY

O JESUS, only-begotten Son of the Eternal Father, well-beloved Son of the Blessed Virgin and foster Child of St. Joseph, we most fervently implore Thee, through Mary Thine ever-blessed Mother and St. Joseph Thy foster father, take our children under Thy special charge and enclose them in the love of Thy Sacred Heart. They are the children of Thy Father in Heaven, created after His own image; they are Thy possession, for Thou hast purchased them with Thy Precious Blood; they are temples of the Holy Ghost, who sanctified them in Baptism and implanted in their hearts the virtues of faith, hope and charity.

O most loving Jesus, rule and guide them, that they may live according to the holy Catholic Faith, that they may not waver in their confidence in Thee and that they may ever remain faithful to Thy love.

O Mary, Blessed Mother of Jesus, grant to our children a place in thy pure maternal heart! Spread over them thy protecting mantle when danger threatens their innocence; keep them firm when they are about to stray from the path of virtue; and should they have the misfortune of falling into mortal sin, oh, then raise them up again, reconcile them with thy Divine Son and restore them to Sanctifying Grace.

And thou, O holy foster father St. Joseph, do not abandon our children! Protect them from the assaults of the wicked enemy and deliver them from all dangers of soul and body.

O dear parents of the holy Child Jesus! Intercede for us parents also, that we may bring up our children in the love and fear of God and one day attain with them the Beatific Vision. Amen.

PRAYER FOR A LIVELY FAITH

O HAPPY, blissful St. Joseph, heir of the faith of all the Patriarchs, vouchsafe to obtain for me this beautiful and precious virtue. Increase in me a lively faith, the foundation of all sanctity, that faith without which no one can be pleasing to God.

Obtain for me that faith which triumphs over all temptations of the world and conquers human respect, which can be shaken by nothing, and which is directed solely toward God. Cause me, after thine example, to live by faith, to subject my heart and understanding to God, that one day I may behold in Heaven what I now firmly believe on earth. Amen.

SEVEN OUR FATHERS . . .

A Devotion of the Pious Union of St. Joseph

IN HONOR of the Seven Sorrows and Seven Joys of St. Joseph, devoutly pray for the dying seven Our Fathers, Hail Marys and Glory be's.

A MORNING OFFERING
THROUGH ST. JOSEPH

RECEIVE me, dear and chosen Father, and the offering of every movement of my body and soul, which I desire to present through thee to my blessed Lord.

Purify all! Make all a perfect holocaust! May every pulsation of my heart be a Spiritual Communion, every look and thought an act of love, every action a sweet sacrifice, every word an arrow of Divine love, every step an advance toward Jesus, every visit to Our Lord as pleasing to God as the errands of Angels, every thought of thee, dear Saint, an act to remind thee that I am your child.

I recommend to thee the occasions in which I usually fail, particularly . . . (*Mention these*). Accept each little devotion of the day, though replete with imperfection, and offer it to Jesus, whose mercy will overlook all, since He regards not so much the gift as the love of the giver. Amen.

Words of Pope Leo XIII

From the Encyclical
Quamquam pluries, August 15, 1889

"Since the bond of marriage existed between Joseph and the Blessed Virgin, there can be no doubt that more than any other person he approached that supereminent dignity by which the Mother of God is raised far above all created natures."

"Blessed Joseph . . . was indeed the husband of Mary and the father, as was supposed, of Jesus Christ. *From this arise all his dignity, grace, holiness and glory* . . . [The Church] is his numberless family, scattered throughout all lands, over which he rules with a sort of paternal authority, because he is the husband of Mary and the father of Jesus Christ."

"Just as Mary, Mother of the Saviour, is spiritual mother of all Christians . . . Joseph looks on all Christians as having been confided to himself . . . He is the defender of the Holy Church, which is truly the House of God and the Kingdom of God on earth."

PRAYER FOR PRIESTS

O ILLUSTRIOUS PATRIARCH St. Joseph, who carried the Infant Jesus in thy blessed arms and who, during the space of thirty years, lived in the most intimate familiarity with Him, take under thy powerful protection those whom He has clothed with His authority and honored with the dignity of His priesthood, whom He has charged to continue His mission, to preach His Gospel, and to dispense everywhere His graces and blessings. Sustain them in their fatigues and labors; console them in their pains; fortify them in their combats; but above all, keep far from them all the evils of sin.

Obtain for them the humility of St. John the Baptist, the faith of St. Peter, the zeal and charity of St. Paul, the purity of St. John and the spirit of prayer and recollection of which thou, my dear Saint, art the model, so that, after having been on earth the faithful dispensers of the Mysteries of thy foster Son, Our Lord Jesus Christ, they may in Heaven receive the recompense promised to pastors according to the Heart of God. Amen.

PRAYER OF CONFIDENCE
IN ST. JOSEPH

By Ven. Martin von Cochem
Based on the Testimony of St. Teresa of Avila

O DEAR ST. JOSEPH, faithful foster father of Jesus Christ, I devoutly come before thy sacred image and implore thine aid and intercession in my present necessity. I know and firmly believe that to thee all things are possible with God, and that the sweet Infant Jesus, who on earth was subject to thee, His reputed father, can now in Heaven refuse thee no request. Thy faithful servant, the seraphic St. Teresa, experienced this and declared that never did she present to thee a petition that thou didst not grant; at the same time she invites all to have recourse to thee, assuring them that they will not depart from thee unconsoled.

Encouraged by this promise, I fly to thee, O holy Joseph, foster father of Jesus Christ and chaste spouse of the Blessed Virgin Mary, beseeching thee by the tender love thou didst bear to both, to bestow on me thy love and mercy. Comfort me in my present trial and affliction and obtain for me, through Jesus and Mary, that God the Father may grant my petition. Send up to the Heart of thy beloved Jesus but a single sigh, lovingly present to Him my request; then I shall certainly obtain it and be consoled in my distress.

To obtain this favor I shall now say three *Our Fathers* and *Hail Marys*.

DAILY PRAYER FOR PROTECTION

By Ven. Martin Von Cochem

HAIL O SAINT JOSEPH! I, thine unworthy child, greet thee. Thou art the faithful protector and intercessor of all who love and venerate thee. Thou knowest that I have special confidence in thee and, after Jesus and Mary, place all my hope of salvation in thee, for thou art all-powerful with God and will never abandon thy faithful servants. Therefore, I humbly invoke thee and commend myself, with all who are dear to me, and my entire possessions, to thy secure protection and powerful intercession. I beseech thee, by the love of Jesus and Mary, do not abandon me during life, and assist me at the hour of my death. Amen.

The Old Testament Joseph

The Great Joseph Who Prefigured an even Greater Joseph

Pharao therefore said to Joseph,

"Thou shalt be over my house, and at the commandment of thy mouth all the people shall obey: only in the kingly throne will I be above thee. And again Pharao said to Joseph: Behold, I have appointed thee over the whole land of Egypt; and he took his ring from his own hand, and gave it into his hand: and he put upon him a robe of silk, and put a chain of gold about his neck. And he made him go up into his second chariot, the crier proclaiming that all should bow their knee before him, and that they should know he was made governor over the whole land of Egypt. And the king said to Joseph: I am Pharao; without thy commandment, no man shall move hand or foot in all the land of Egypt; and he turned his name, and called him in the Egyptian tongue, The saviour of the world . . . Now when the seven years of the plenty that had been in Egypt were past, the seven years of scarcity, which Joseph had foretold, began to come: and the famine prevailed in the whole world, but there was bread in all the land of Egypt. And when there also they began to be famished, the people cried to Pharao for food. And he said to them: 'Go to Joseph: and do all that he shall say to you.' And the famine increased daily in all the land: and Joseph opened all the barns, and sold to the Egyptians: for the famine had oppressed them also. And all provinces came into Egypt to buy food, and to seek some relief of their want."—*Genesis* 41:40-45, 53-57.

The Two Josephs

The chaste Joseph of the Old Testament was a prototype of St. Joseph, the foster father of Our Lord. Pharao raised him from his humble position in life to the highest dignity in the land and directed all his subjects to apply to Joseph in their needs, saying, *Ite ad Joseph*—"Go to Joseph!" (*Gen.* 11:55).

In the same words Holy Church and the Vicar of Christ direct the faithful to have recourse to St. Joseph in all their spiritual and temporal necessities.

TRIDUUM FOR
THE GAINING OF
SOME SPECIAL GRACE
—The "Go to Joseph" Prayer—

I

IN the miseries of this vale of tears, to whom shall we have recourse, O blessed Joseph, if not to thee, to whom thy beloved spouse Mary entrusted all her rich treasures, that thou might keep them to our advantage? "Go to my spouse, Joseph," Mary seems to say to us, "and he will comfort you, he will deliver you from the misfortunes which now oppress you and will make you happy and contented." Have pity on us, therefore, O St. Joseph; have pity on us through that love which thou didst cherish toward a spouse so worthy and so amiable.

Our Father . . . Hail Mary . . . Glory be . . .

II

We are fully conscious that we have offended the justice of God by our sins and deserve His most severe chastisements. Now what shall be our place of refuge? In what haven shall we find ourselves in safety? "Go to Joseph," Jesus seems to say to us; "Go to Joseph, in whom I was well pleased and whom I had for My foster father. To him, as to a father, I have communicated all power, that he may use it for your good according to his own desire." Pity us, therefore, O blessed Joseph, pity us, for the great love thou didst bear toward a Son so admirable and so dear.

Our Father . . . Hail Mary . . . Glory be . . .

III

Unhappily, the sins we have committed call down upon us the heaviest scourges: this we must confess. In what ark shall we take refuge in order to be saved? Where shall we find the blessed rainbow that shall give us comfort and hope in the midst of our affliction? "Go to Joseph," the Eternal Father seems to say to us: "Go to him who took My place on earth with regard to My Son made man. I entrusted to his keeping My Son, who is the unfailing source of grace; therefore, every grace is in his hands." Pity us, then, dear St. Joseph, pity us by thy great love for Almighty God, who has been so generous to thee.

Our Father . . . Hail Mary . . . Glory be . . .

A Father to the Poor

Again and again the Church compares St. Joseph's position with that of Joseph of Egypt in the house of Pharaoh. We know that Joseph of Egypt was the generous benefactor of whole nations. How many people would have perished during the seven years of famine had not Joseph, through his wisdom and foresight, provided that the superabundance of seven good years be stored away. Thus the king could satisfy all petitioners for food, for he had merely to say: "Go to Joseph."

But to the glorious St. Joseph God has given still greater power to help the poor. How good and powerful St. Joseph is in this regard can be shown especially by the experiences of numerous convents and religious orders. Many who were poor themselves accomplished wonderful things by placing their trust in St. Joseph. With his aid they built churches, schools, convents and charitable institutions of every description. How many instances could here be mentioned in which St. Joseph miraculously came to the aid of convents and religious communities in cases of dire poverty! With his assistance, St. Teresa of Avila founded more than 20 convents.

One day this Saint was in great perplexity because she had no money wherewith to pay the laborers, and she saw no way out of her embarrassment. Thereupon, St. Joseph appeared to her and offered to go security for her and also to be her treasurer. He promised her that money should be at hand, induced her to make an agreement with the laborers regarding their wages and to continue the work with more energy than ever. Although St. Teresa had not a farthing, she nevertheless did as St. Joseph told her, and in so extraordinary a manner did she receive aid that all who knew of it were greatly astonished.

St. Joseph, however, aids not only the religious *but all the poor who take refuge in him with confidence.* Many examples are recorded in which he has come to the assistance of the poor and needy in a most wonderful manner. The poor should especially venerate and invoke St. Joseph when in trouble; he will not let their trust in him be confounded. While on earth, St. Joseph himself experienced the hardships of poverty, and therefore he is now so good and powerful a patron of the poor.

St. Joseph's Liberality

Our Lord permits St. Joseph to take from His Divine treasury with full hands in order to give to souls the treasures of Divine grace and mercy, like Joseph, the son of Jacob, who took corn from the granaries of the King of Egypt to feed his brethren and all who had recourse to him. From the heights of Heaven, the King of Glory speaks to us the same words as Pharao spoke to the starving people of Egypt: "Go to Joseph!"

NOVENA IN SPECIAL NECESSITIES

O HOLY JOSEPH, thou who hast never been invoked in vain, whose arms are ever open to receive the poor afflicted who have recourse to thee, whose heart is ever accessible to those who seek refuge with thee, mercifully cast a glance of pity on my great misery. Thou knowest the great trial that God sees fit to send me; thou knowest the excessive grief that fills my heart. The cross weighs heavily on my shoulders, "for the hand of the Lord hath touched me."

In vain have I raised my voice to the throne of the Divine Majesty; the Lord seems not to hearken to my petitions. I have indeed deserved these trials, these temptations, these afflictions, for I have sinned and therefore I must suffer. But do thou, O St. Joseph, whose influence with God is so great, do thou, beloved father, make intercession for me with Jesus. Oh, be my advocate with thy Divine Son, whose protector, foster father and solicitous guardian thou hast been. Add to thy great glory also this, that thou wilt give aid in the hopeless affairs which I now commend to thee.

I believe, yes, I believe that thou canst deliver me from my afflictions and will grant my petition.

I have unshaken confidence that thou wilt leave nothing undone to assist one in darkness who humbly and fervently asks thy help. Behold me here at thy feet, O good St. Joseph! Look upon me, have pity on my sighs and tears. Do not abandon me; I will not depart until thou hast spread over me the mantle of thy compassion and promised me thine intercession with God.

Then ask St. Joseph's blessing:

Petition for St. Joseph's Blessing

Bless me, O dearly beloved Father, St. Joseph; bless my body and my soul; bless my resolutions, my words and deeds, all my actions and omissions, my every step; bless all that I possess, all my interior and exterior goods, that all may redound to the greater honor of God. Bless me for time and eternity, and preserve me from every sin.

Obtain for me the grace to make atonement for all my sins by love and contrition here on earth, so that after my last breath I may, without delay, prostrate at your feet, return thee thanks in Heaven for all the love and goodness thou, O dearest father, hast shown me here below. Amen.

Now pray the Our Father, Hail Mary and Glory be to the Father three times, in thanksgiving to God for the graces and prerogatives bestowed on St. Joseph.

Offering

O Jesus, Mary and Joseph, accept these three *Our Fathers* from me, a poor sinner, and grant that my prayer may be pleasing to thee. Let my sighs penetrate to thy hearts, that my petition may be favorably received.

I beseech thee by the faithful love which thou hadst for one another, and by all the compassion thou ever showed to those in distress, show thy love also to me in my present need, and grant my earnest petition. (*Name your request.*)

ACT OF CONSECRATION TO ST. JOSEPH

O DEAREST St. Joseph, I consecrate myself to thy honor and give myself to thee, that thou mayest always be my father, my protector and my guide in the way of salvation. Obtain for me a great purity of heart and a fervent love of the interior life. After thine example, may I do all my actions for the greater glory of God, in union with the Divine Heart of Jesus and the Immaculate Heart of Mary! And do thou, O blessed St. Joseph, pray for me that I may share in the peace and joy of thy holy death. Amen.

St. Joseph's Virtues

Words of Our Lady to St. Bridget of Sweden

"St. Joseph was so reserved and careful in his speech that not one word ever issued from his mouth that was not good and holy, nor did he ever indulge in unnecessary or less than charitable conversation. He was most patient and diligent in bearing fatigue; he practiced extreme poverty; he was most meek in bearing injuries; he was strong and constant against my enemies; he was the faithful witness of the wonders of Heaven, being dead to the flesh and the world, living only for God and for heavenly goods, which were the only things he desired. He was perfectly conformed to the Divine Will and so resigned to the dispositions of Heaven that he ever repeated: 'May the Will of God ever be done in me!' He rarely spoke with men, but continually with God, whose Will he desired to perform. Wherefore, he now enjoys great glory in Heaven."

ANOTHER ACT OF CONSECRATION TO ST. JOSEPH

O BLESSED JOSEPH, foster father of my Saviour and chaste spouse of the Mother of God, this day I irrevocably adopt thee for my intercessor with the Almighty as well as my model, my protector and my father in this valley of exile. O St. Joseph, whom the Lord constituted guardian of His Family, I beseech thee to extend thy tender solicitude over all my interests. Kindle in my heart a vehement love for Jesus and enable me to serve Him with all thy devotedness and fidelity. Aid my inability to venerate Mary as my advocate, to honor her as my Queen and to love her as my Mother. Be my never-failing guide in the way of virtue and piety, and grant that, after having faithfully followed thee in the path of justice, I may receive thy powerful protection at the hour of my death. Amen.

PETITION AND OFFERING TO ST. JOSEPH

O GREAT St. Joseph, generous depository and dispenser of immortal riches, behold us prostrate at thy feet, earnestly beseeching thee to receive us as thy servants and thy children. Next to the Sacred Heart of Jesus and the Immaculate Heart of Mary, of which thou art the faithful copy, we acknowledge that there is no heart more tender, more compassionate, than thine. What, then, have we to fear—or rather, for what should we not hope, if thou dost deign to be our benefactor, our master, our model, our father and our mediator?

Refuse not, then, this favor, O powerful Protector! We ask it of thee by the love thou dost bear to Jesus and Mary. Into thy hands we commit our souls and our bodies, but above all, the last moments of our lives. May we, after having honored, imitated and served thee on earth, eternally sing with thee the mercies of Jesus and Mary. Amen.

O holy St. Joseph, we give thanks to God for the signal favors conferred on thee, and we beg thy intercession to help us imitate thy virtues. Pray for us, O great Saint, that we may be humble, patient

and trustful like thee; and by that love which thou
hast for Jesus and Mary, and the love they have for
thee, obtain for us the grace to live and die in their
love. Amen.

The Vision of St. Gertrude

Once, on the feast of the Annunciation, St. Gertrude had
a vision during which the Heavenly Mother revealed to her
the glory of her spouse, St. Joseph, in order to awaken in
the Saint a greater love for him and to encourage her to have
confidence in his intercession. Of this vision St. Gertrude
wrote:

"I saw Heaven opened and St. Joseph sitting upon a mag-
nificent throne. I felt myself wonderfully affected when,
each time his name was mentioned, all the Saints made a
profound inclination toward him, showing by the serenity
and sweetness of their looks that they rejoiced with him on
account of his exalted dignity."

AN ACT OF OFFERING TO OUR PATRIARCH ST. JOSEPH

O MOST GLORIOUS PATRIARCH, chaste spouse of the great Mother of God and reputed father of my Lord Jesus Christ, my loving St. Joseph, confiding in the greatness of thy holiness and inflamed with the love which Jesus and Mary bore thee, I choose thee this day, in their presence, to be my special protector, advocate and patron, and I firmly propose to keep this devotion to thee always burning within my heart. And since I know that thou wast appointed by the Eternal Father to be the head of the Holy Family upon earth, and I desire to be one of its devoted servants and friends, I beg of thee to admit me into that number. I beseech thee also, O my most glorious father St. Joseph, to obtain for me, through thy great merits and by thy most powerful intercession, the grace to imitate in my life thy most holy conversation with Jesus and Mary, so that I too, like thyself, may enjoy the assistance of Jesus and Mary at my death, and in their arms may breathe forth my soul, saying, "Jesus, Mary and Joseph, I give thee my heart and my soul." Amen.

Patron of a Happy Death

It is undeniable that St. Joseph is a special protector of his dying clients and all those in their last agony. This has been experienced by numberless persons who practiced special devotion to St. Joseph during life. At the hour of death, man is subject to untold suffering and anguish. At that supreme moment, every Christian must undergo a terrible trial, upon the final outcome of which depends eternal joy or endless woe. The fury of Hell, the remembrance of past sins, the uncertainty of the future, the pains of death, the terror of the Judgment—all these are sources of untold sufferings. *What Saint could defend us better than St. Joseph, whom the whole Christian world acknowledges as the protector and patron of the dying!*

There are three reasons why St. Joseph is a special patron of the dying: 1) He is the foster father of the Eternal Judge, who can refuse him no request. 2) He is terrible to the demons; the Church calls him the *Terror of demons* and *Conqueror of Hell*. 3) His own death was most beautiful, for he died in the arms of Jesus and Mary. This is the principal reason why he is the patron of a happy death; the death of no other Saint was so happy, so glorious. St. Francis de Sales was of the opinion that St. Joseph died of the love of God; St. Alphonsus Liguori considered this view most reasonable. Ven. Mary of Agreda says that before his death St. Joseph experienced a rapture which lasted 24 hours, during which he beheld the Divine Essence, the Face of God, His glory, which Moses had in vain asked to see. (Ex. 33:18, 20). Jesus and Mary together closed St. Joseph's eyes in death and shed tears at his departure. If Jesus wept over Lazarus, how must He have wept over St. Joseph!

Wonderful examples could be cited from the lives of many ordinary Christians of how *St. Joseph obtained for them a happy death* because during life they had prayed to him for this grace.

Let us daily ask him to assist us at the hour of death and remind him of his own glorious departure in the arms of Jesus and Mary.

PRAYER FOR A HAPPY DEATH

O GLORIOUS St. Joseph, behold I choose thee today for my special patron in life and at the hour of my death. Preserve and increase in me the spirit of prayer and fervor in the service of God. Remove far from me every kind of sin; obtain for me that my death may not come upon me unawares, but that I may have time to confess my sins sacramentally and to bewail them with a most

perfect understanding and a most sincere and perfect contrition, in order that I may breathe forth my soul into the hands of Jesus and Mary. Amen.

ANOTHER PRAYER FOR A HAPPY DEATH

O BLESSED JOSEPH, who yielded up thy last breath in the arms of Jesus and Mary, obtain for me, I beseech thee, the grace of a happy death. Defend me from the attacks of my enemy in that hour of pain and anguish, to which I now invite thee, that thou mayest assist me by thy presence and protect me by thy power.

Obtain for me this grace, O holy Joseph, that I may breathe forth my soul in praise, saying in spirit, if I am unable to do so in words: "Jesus, Mary and Joseph, I give thee my heart and my soul." Amen.

THE NINE FIRST WEDNESDAYS

A devotion propagated by the Pious Union of St. Joseph

Every Wednesday is dedicated in a special way to St. Joseph. Make the Nine First Wednesdays (in a manner similar to the First Fridays) in honor of St. Joseph for a happy death for yourself and your dear ones. As charity is one of the best ways to be worthy of the grace of a happy death, offer your First Wednesday Mass and Communion and devotions in honor of St. Joseph in a special way for the salvation of the dying.

The Body and Tomb of St. Joseph

"In an ecstasy, a Saint has seen the body of St. Joseph preserved intact in a tomb, the site of which is yet unknown. The more the glorious spouse of the most Blessed Virgin is honored, the sooner will the finding of his body take place, which will be a day of great joy for the Church." (Words of Father Paul of Moll, 1824-1896, from *Father Paul of Moll*, by Edward van Speybrouck, p. 238).

An ancient tradition states that the tomb of St. Joseph, now empty, is in the Valley of Josaphat. St. Jerome, on the other hand, was of the opinion that St. Joseph's tomb is within the boundaries of the Garden of Gethsemane. (See *Life and Glories of St. Joseph*, by Edward Healy Thompson, pp. 409-410).

The answer to these questions remains a mystery at this time.

PRAYER FOR A GOOD LIFE
AND A HAPPY DEATH

O GLORIOUS St. Joseph, spouse of the Immaculate Virgin, obtain for me a pure, humble and charitable mind and perfect resignation to the Divine Will. Be my guide, father, and model through life, that I may merit to die as thou didst die, in the arms of Jesus and Mary. Amen.

Words of St. Alphonsus Liguori

"Since we all must die, we should cherish a special devotion to St. Joseph, that he may obtain for us a happy death. All Christians regard him as the advocate of the dying who had honored him during their life, and that for three reasons:

"First, because Jesus Christ loved him not only as a friend, but as a father, and on this account his mediation is far more efficacious than that of any other Saint.

"Second, because St. Joseph has obtained special power against the evil spirits, who tempt us with redoubled vigor at the hour of death.

"Third, the assistance given St. Joseph at his death by Jesus and Mary obtained for him the right to secure a holy and peaceful death for his servants. Hence, if they invoke him at the hour of death *he will not only help them, but he will also obtain for them the assistance of Jesus and Mary.*"

PETITION FOR OUR DYING MOMENTS

O GLORIOUS ST. JOSEPH, whom I contemplate dying between Jesus and Mary, obtain for me, as well as for all those who are dear to me, the grace of leading a life like thine, so that we may die, like thee, the death of the just, assisted in our last struggle by our Divine Saviour and His most holy Mother.

O St. Joseph, holy patron of a good death, I take refuge at the foot of thy altar to implore thee to succor me at the moment when the Sovereign Judge will call me to appear in His presence. When my eyes shall be ready to close to the light of this world, when my tongue shall only with difficulty be able to repeat the names of Jesus and Mary, come then to me: Come to present my soul to God, who wished to be as a son to thee, and obtain that the sentence He shall pronounce over me may make me a partaker of the glory thou dost enjoy forever in Heaven. Amen.

PRAYER TO JESUS, MARY AND JOSEPH FOR A HAPPY DEATH

O MY DEAREST and most beloved Jesus, Who sacrificed everything, even Thy life, that my soul should not be lost, be to me a *Jesus*[1] in my last hour, and deliver my soul from the power of her enemies. Alas, weak and wretched sinner that I am, who have fallen into so many temptations, how shall I endure my final struggle and escape the last temptations of the wicked enemy if Thou, O my Jesus, shall desert me and put not the evil one to flight?

By Thy dereliction on the Cross for me and by Thine agony of death for me, I earnestly beseech Thee, O Jesus, do not abandon me in my last agony, lest I be overcome by faint-heartedness. Strengthen my faith, support my hope, preserve and increase my charity, and grant me the grace to yield my spirit with perfect resignation into the hands of Thy Heavenly Father, that I may not be rejected, but may obtain a favorable and merciful Judgment. Oh, do not permit that Thy Precious Blood, Thy bitter Passion and Death shall have been offered in vain for me!

O Mary, most tender Virgin and the Mother of Jesus, Health of the sick, Hope of the dying, behold how miserable and poor I am! Come to my assistance in my distress, O Comforter of the Afflicted, and comfort my heart also. After God, thou art my surest hope, and I firmly believe that God cannot cast me away as long as thou art my Mother and art solicitous for me; yes, I believe that I cannot be lost if I hold fast to thee.

O my loving Mother, do not let my confidence be confounded. With all possible fidelity I commend to thee my poor soul and enclose it in thy most sweet Mother's heart—not only now, but especially in my last agony, when I shall be abandoned by the world. Remember me then; come to my aid when my strength fails me, when my terror increases and my tongue is no longer able to pronounce the holy Name of Jesus and thine own consoling name, O beloved Mother. Remember then my earnest pleading, and let my poor soul experience thy tender care, that I may arrive happily at the end of my earthly pilgrimage.

O St. Joseph, faithful foster father of Christ, appointed by God as a special patron of the dying, as such does Holy Church venerate thee. I therefore invoke thee in my distress and commend to thee my departure from this world.

O dear St. Joseph, obtain for me the grace that I too may have the inexpressible happiness of dying assisted by Jesus and Mary. O dear Saint, when my soul is seized with fear in the agony of its last struggle, call upon thy Divine Foster Child and thy most holy Spouse, that the evil one may not approach, and that my soul may depart in peace. Amen.

A SHORT PRAYER FOR THE DYING

The special prayer of the Pious Union of St. Joseph

O ST. JOSEPH, foster father of the Child Jesus and true spouse of the Blessed Virgin Mary, pray for us and for the dying of this day (or *of this night*). Amen.

PRAYER FOR THE AGONIZING

O ST. JOSEPH, protector of those in agony, take pity on those who at this very moment when I pray to thee are engaged in their last combat.

O blessed Joseph, take pity on my soul too when the hour of the final battle shall arrive for me. Then, O my holy patron, do not abandon me, but grant me thine assistance; show that thou art my good father, and obtain that my Divine Saviour may receive me with mercy into that abode where the elect enjoy a life that shall never end. Amen.

PRAYER FOR SOULS IN THE AGONY OF DEATH

E TERNAL Father, by the love Thou bearest toward St. Joseph, who was chosen by Thee from among all men to exercise Thy divine fatherhood over Thy Son made Man, have mercy on us and upon all poor souls who are in their agony.

Our Father . . . Hail Mary . . . Glory be . . .

Eternal Son of God, by the love Thou bearest toward St. Joseph, who was Thy most faithful guardian upon earth, have mercy on us and upon all poor souls who are in their agony.

Our Father . . . Hail Mary . . . Glory be . . .

Eternal Spirit of God, by the love Thou bearest toward St. Joseph, who guarded with such tender care most holy Mary, Thy beloved spouse, have mercy on us and upon all poor souls who are in their agony.

Our Father . . . Hail Mary . . . Glory be . . .

St. Joseph's Intercession

As foster father of Jesus and spouse of the Virgin Mother, St. Joseph enjoys a unique splendor and a power of intercession far above that of every other Saint except Our Lady. Except for the Blessed Virgin, who can plead with Jesus more effectually than St. Joseph? For if Jesus was obedient to him during His earthly life, will He not now delight to hearken with a special readiness to St. Joseph's pleadings on behalf of those who have recourse to him?

Inexpressibly great, therefore, is St. Joseph's power of intercession in Heaven; inexpressibly great is also his love for us, his charges here on earth. For this reason let us place boundless confidence in him in all the affairs of life.

JESUS, MARY AND JOSEPH

JESUS, Mary and Joseph, I give thee my heart and
my soul.

Jesus, Mary and Joseph, assist me in my last
agony.

Jesus, Mary and Joseph, may I breathe forth my
soul in peace with thee.

LITANY TO ST. JOSEPH
FOR A DYING PERSON

(For private use only.)

LORD, have mercy on us.
  Christ, have mercy on us.
Lord, have mercy on us. Christ, hear us.
  Christ, graciously hear us.
God the Father of Heaven,
  have mercy on us.
God the Son, Redeemer of the world,
  have mercy on us.
God the Holy Ghost, *etc.*
Holy Trinity, one God,

St. Joseph, foster father of Christ,
  we beseech thee, hear us.
St. Joseph, patron of the dying,
  we beseech thee, hear us.
Obtain for him (her) forgiveness of his
  (her) sins, *etc.*
Obtain for him (her) great patience,
Obtain for him a perfect resignation,
Obtain for him a living and unshaken faith,
Obtain for him a firm confidence,
Obtain for him ardent charity,
Avert from him the attacks of the enemy,
Protect him from the temptations that
  assail him,
Preserve him from despondency and despair,
Obtain for him the grace of Jesus Christ,
Assist him and do not abandon him,
Come to his aid in his weakness,
Assist him in his abandonment,
Obtain for him a happy death,
Obtain for him a merciful judgment,

Conduct his soul to the vision of Jesus,
  there to obtain mercy for him. *Amen.*

PIOUS INVOCATIONS

(To be pronounced in the presence of a dying person.)

O GOD, be gracious to me; O God, have mercy on me; O God, forgive me my sins!

O God the Father, have mercy on me; O Jesus, be gracious to me; O Holy Spirit, strengthen me!

O God the Father, do not reject me; O Jesus, do not abandon me; O God the Holy Spirit, do not forsake me!

O my God, into Thy hands I commend my spirit; O Jesus, Son of David, have mercy on me! O Jesus, Son of Mary, have mercy on me!

O Jesus, I believe in Thee; O Jesus, I hope in Thee; O Jesus, I love Thee!

O Jesus, I place all my trust in Thy bitter Passion!

O Jesus, in Thy Sacred Wounds I hide myself!

O Jesus, I enclose myself in Thy Sacred Heart!

Holy Mary, Mother of God, assist me!

Holy Mary, protect me from the evil spirit!

Holy Mary, turn thine eyes of mercy upon me!

O Mary, Mother of mercy, obtain grace for me from thy dear Son!

Come to my aid, O Mary, in this my anguish and need!

O Mary, enclose me in thy virginal heart!

O Mary, commend me to thy Son, present me to thy Son, reconcile me with thy Son!

St. Joseph, obtain for me grace and mercy!

St. Joseph, assist me in my struggle against the enemy of my salvation!

St. Joseph, to thee do I entrust my soul: do thou save it for me!

St. Joseph, remember me, and obtain mercy for me!

O holy Guardian Angel, do not abandon me, but combat for me and preserve me from the evil one!

My dear Patron Saints, pray for me!

Jesus, Jesus, Jesus, into Thy hands I commend my spirit!

PRAYER FOR A HEAVENLY CROWN

O ST. JOSEPH, virgin father of Jesus and most pure spouse of the Blessed Virgin Mary, pray every day for us to the same Jesus, the Son of God, that being defended by the power of His grace and striving dutifully in life, we may be crowned by Him at the hour of death. Amen.

PRAYER BEFORE MASS AND HOLY COMMUNION

Prayer especially for priests, based on the praise of St. Joseph by St. Bernard of Clairvaux.

O BLESSED JOSEPH, happy man, to whom it was given not only to see and to hear that God whom many kings longed to see, and saw not, to hear, and heard not; but also to carry Him in thine arms, to embrace Him, to clothe Him and to guard and defend Him.

V. Pray for us, O blessed Joseph.

R. That we may be made worthy of the promises of Christ.

Let Us Pray

O God, Who has given unto us a royal priesthood, we beseech Thee that as blessed Joseph was found worthy to touch with his hands and to bear in his arms Thine Only-begotten Son, born of the Virgin Mary, so may we be made fit, by cleanness of heart and blamelessness of life, to minister at Thy holy altar; may we this day partake with reverent devotion of the Sacred Body and Blood of Thine Only-begotten Son, and may we in the world to come be accounted worthy of receiving an everlasting reward. Through the same Christ Our Lord. Amen.

THE CHAPLET OF ST. JOSEPH

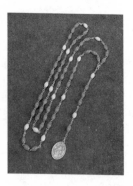

THIS chaplet is divided into 15 groups of four beads consisting of one white and three purple beads. The white beads symbolize St. Joseph's purity, and the purple his saintly piety. On each white bead a Mystery of the Rosary is considered and two Hail Marys are said.

On the purple beads, say

Praised and blessed be Jesus, Mary and Joseph.

The chaplet is ended with the following:

V. Pray for us, O holy St. Joseph,
R. That we may be made worthy of the promises of Christ.

Let Us Pray

O God, Who predestined St. Joseph from all eternity for the service of Thine Eternal Son and His Blessed Mother, and made him worthy to be the spouse of this Blessed Virgin and the foster father of Thy Son, we beseech Thee, through all the services he rendered to Jesus and Mary on earth, do Thou make us worthy of his intercession on earth and grant us to enjoy the happiness of his company in Heaven, through Christ our Lord. Amen.

THE CORD OF ST. JOSEPH

THE Cord of St. Joseph originated in Antwerp, Belgium, in 1657 with the miraculous cure of a devout Augustinian nun named Sister Elizabeth. After a severe and painful illness of three years' duration, the physicians had given up hope of curing her and expected her soon to die. But Sister Elizabeth, having always been devoted to St. Joseph, made a cord, had it blessed in the Saint's honor and put it around her waist. A few days later, when praying before his statue, she was suddenly freed from pain. Her recovery was considered miraculous. Eventually the devotion of the Cord spread, and numerous special graces were obtained through its devout use. The Cord was used not merely as a remedy against bodily ailments, but also as a spiritual aid to preserve the virtue of purity. The devotion was approved by the Sacred Congregation of Rites on September 19, 1859, and it was also blessed and approved by Pope Pius IX.

Graces obtained by the wearing of this Cord are 1) St. Joseph's special protection; 2) purity of soul; 3) the grace of chastity; 4) final perseverance; 5) particular assistance at the hour of death.

The Cord should be of thread or cotton, with seven knots at one end, and should be worn around the waist. It should be blessed by a priest.

One who wears the Cord should recite the *Glory be to the Father* seven times daily in honor of St. Joseph, together with the Prayer for Purity on p. 19.

A Catholic Custom

It is a pious custom often followed by Catholics to attach to an image of St. Joseph a note with one's petition written on it. The note serves as a continual petition to St. Joseph, much like a candle lighted before a sacred image. It also makes concrete, and thus strengthens, our confidence in St. Joseph—and confidence obtains all.

The Little Sisters of the Poor, who care for the elderly poor, have received many favors from St. Joseph after placing in front of his statue a sample of the object they needed or would like for the dear residents of their homes: a potato, a lump of coal, even a can of beer; in one way or another, these things are obtained.

In 1977 a hospitality kitchen and clinic run by a Catholic community in Los Angeles needed $64,000 to purchase the building they were renting. After receiving an eviction notice, they set out to raise the money. At this time, Mother Teresa of Calcutta happened to visit; she told the community to petition St. Joseph—and to write out their petition and tie it to a statue of St. Joseph. Feeling a little strange about this, the community members nevertheless got the pastor's permission and tied a note to the finger of the statue of St. Joseph at a local parish. And they prayed. Within two weeks, they had received $55,000, with the largest gift, $5,000, coming from someone in Alaska whom they did not even know.

The realtor called it "the craziest deal I ever heard of." (See *Our Sunday Visitor*, August 21, 1977).

OUR FATHER

OUR FATHER, Who art in Heaven, hallowed be Thy Name. Thy kingdom come, Thy will be done on earth as it is in Heaven. Give us this day our daily bread, and forgive us our trespasses, as we forgive those who trespass against us. And lead us not into temptation, but deliver us from evil. Amen.

HAIL MARY

HAIL MARY, full of grace, the Lord is with thee; blessed art thou among women, and blessed is the fruit of thy womb, Jesus. Holy Mary, Mother of God, pray for us sinners, now and at the hour of our death. Amen.

GLORY BE

GLORY BE to the Father, and to the Son, and to the Holy Ghost. As it was in the beginning, is now, and ever shall be, world without end. Amen.

BLESSING OF ST. JOSEPH

MAY the poverty of my sweet and suffering little Child be your riches; His sighs and tears, the consolation of your days; the love of His infant Heart, all your earthly treasure; and the clear vision of His adorable and glorified humanity, your eternal joy and recompense. Amen.

BLESSING OF ST. JOSEPH

MAY the poverty of my sweet and suffering little Child be your riches; His sighs and tears, the consolation of your days; the love of His infant Heart, all your earthly treasure; and the clean vision of His adorable and glorified humanity, your eternal joy and recompense. Amen.

GREAT ST. JOSEPH,
SON OF DAVID

1. Great Saint Jo-seph, son of Da-vid, Fos-ter fa-ther of our Lord,
2. Three long days, in grief, in an-guish, With that Moth-er sweet and mild,

Spouse of Ma-ry ev-er Vir-gin, Keep-ing o'er them watch and ward:
Ma-ry Vir-gin, didst thou wan-der, Seek-ing her be-lov-ed Child.

In the sta-ble thou didst guard them With a fa-ther's lov-ing care;
In the tem-ple thou didst find Him: O what joy then filled thy heart!

Thou by God's command didst save them From the cru-el Her-od's snare.
In thy sor-rows, in thy glad-ness, Grant us, Jo-seph, to have part.

3. Clasped in Jesus' arms and Mary's,
   When death gently came at last,
   Thy pure spirit, sweetly sighing,
   From its earthly dwelling passed.
   Dear Saint Joseph, by that passing,
   May our death be like to thine,
   And with Jesus, Mary, Joseph,
   May our souls forever shine.

SALVE PATER SALVATORIS

Text: Vss 1&2, trad/Vs. 3 Nancy Llewellyn

Thomas F. Savoy, b. 1955

Sal - ve Pa - ter Sal - va - to - ris, Sal - ve cus - tos Re - demp - to - ris,

O Jo - seph a - ma - bi - lis, Sal - ve! Sal - ve!

1. Sal ve Pa - ter Je - su me - i, Spon - se Ge - ni - tri - cis De - i,
2. Pi - um Pi - us te Pa - tro - num, Te tu - to - rem de - dit fi - dum
3. Vir - gi - num tu - ta - men no - tum Spe - cu - lum - que Sa - cer - do - tum

Quem de - co - rat pu - ri - tas,
Pon - ti - fex Ec - cle - si - ae, Sal - ve! Sal - ve!
Te - ne - bra - rum ful - mi - na!